no
Indian
cooking

Devagi Sanmugam

Delicious recipes from the northern provinces of the
spicy subcontinent—including favourites like
Tandoori Naan, Saffron Rice, Chicken Tikka and Prawn Briyani.

PERIPLUS

Basic North Indian Ingredients

Basmati rice is an Indian long-grain rice characterised by its thinness and fragrance. The grains stay whole and separate when cooked with oil and spices. Substitute with long-grain Thai jasmine rice.

Cardamom is a highly aromatic pod containing tiny black seeds. If whole pods are used, they should be removed from the food before serving. If seeds are called for, lightly smash the pods and remove the seeds. Ground cardamon is sold in packets or tins.

Carom seeds are from the same family as cumin and parsley, and are known as *ajwain* in India. The seeds are similar in appearance and flavour to caraway seeds, but with strong overtones of thyme. Look for this in Indian specialty stores.

Channa flour is made by milling hulled Indian brown chickpeas. It is very fine in texture and pale yellow in colour. It can be obtained from Indian grocers, gourmet and health-food stores. Finely ground chickpea flour may be used as a substitute.

Chillies are indispensable in Asian cooking. The commonly-used red and green finger-length chillies are moderately hot. Dried chillies are usually cut in lengths and soaked in warm water to soften before use.

Chilli powder, a crucial ingredient in Indian cooking, is a hot seasoning made from ground chillies.

Cumin seeds (*jeera*) are pale brown and usually partnered with coriander seeds in basic spice mixes. They impart an intense, earthy flavour to foods and are often dry-roasted or flash-cooked in oil to intensify their flavour.

Curry leaves are sold in sprigs containing 8–15 small, green leaves and are used to flavour Indian curries. There is no good substitute.

Curry powder is a readily available blend of Indian spice, and typically contains turmeric, coriander, chillies, cumin, mustard, ginger, fenugreek, garlic, cloves, salt, and any number of other spices.

Dal refers to a wide variety of split peas and pulses. Several kinds are used in these recipes. **Channa dal** or Bengal gram resembles a yellow split pea but is smaller. **Mung dal** is the split version of the same bean used to make bean sprouts. It is pale yellow and slightly elongated. **Urad dal** or **blackgram dal** is sold either with its black skin on or husked, when it is creamy white in colour. **Red** and **pigeon lentils** are also used and can be found in Indian foodstores, supermarkets and health food stores.

Fennel is similar in appearance to cumin although slightly longer and fatter. Fennel has a sweet fragrance that is similar to aniseed. The seeds are used whole or ground.

Fenugreek is an almost square, hard, yellowish-brown seed. It is strongly flavoured and easily available from Asian foodstores and supermarkets. The taste is somewhat like burnt maple, sweet yet bitter, with a hint of celery. In addition to curries, fenugreek will enhance meats, poultry and vegetables. Too much of it will cause foods to become bitter, so use with caution.

Fenugreek leaves are a mildly bitter herb that is believed to have medicinal properties. Dried leaves,

either whole or ground, are called *kasuri methi*, and they're a good substitute for fresh. Look for fresh or dried leaves in Indian markets. If unavailable, substitute celery leaves.

Garam masala is an Indian blend of powdered spices, usually including cinnamon, cardamon, cloves, fennel and black pepper. Pre-blended *garam masala* can be bought from any store specializing in spices. Store the ground powder in an airtight jar away from heat or sunlight.

Ghee is a rich clarified butter oil with the milk solids removed that is the main oil used in Indian cooking. Substitute with vegetable oil or butter.

Mustard seeds are small brownish-black seeds that are commonly used in Indian cooking, imparting a nutty flavour to dishes.

Mustard oil is vegetable oil infused with ground

mustard seeds and used for cooking as well as preserving. The flavour is distinct and is worth looking for in Indian specialty stores; if unavailable, substitute any refined vegetable oil.

Saffron is the world's most expensive spice. The dried strands should be allowed to infuse in warm milk before being added to rice and dessert dishes. Store saffron in the freezer as it loses its fragrance quickly, and never buy powdered saffron if you want the true aroma of this spice.

Turmeric root is a member of the ginger family. It is sold as a dried root or in powdered form. Purchase turmeric as you need it as the flavour can fade over time. Adjust according to taste but be aware that turmeric is quite pungent. Be careful, as it can also stain clothing and plastic utensils.

Ketchumbar (Cucumber and Tomato Salad with Coriander Mint Dressing)

2 medium cucumbers, seeded and diced to yield 375 g ($2^1/_2$ cups)
2 medium or 3 small tomatoes, seeded and diced
2 tablespoons finely chopped mint leaves
1 tablespoon finely chopped coriander leaves
100 ml ($^1/_3$ cup) freshly squeezed lemon juice
$^1/_2$ teaspoon salt
$^1/_2$ teaspoon sugar
1 green finger-length chilli, seeded and sliced

1 Put the cucumber, tomato, mint and coriander leaves into a serving bowl.
2 Mix the rest of the ingredients until the sugar dissolves, pour onto the salad ingredients, toss and serve immediately.

Serves 4–6
Preparation time: 20 mins

Fruit Salad Raita

1 medium banana, cubed
1 mandarin orange, peeled and cubed
1 ripe mango, peeled and cubed
200 g ($1^1/_2$ cups) seedless grapes, halved
1 large green apple, cored and cubed
2 tablespoons chopped coriander leaves
300 ml ($1^1/_4$ cups) plain yoghurt
$1^1/_2$ teaspoons sugar
$^1/_2$ teaspoon salt
2 teaspoons lemon juice
1 red finger-length chilli, sliced
$^1/_2$ teaspoon roasted cumin seeds, pounded coarsely

1 Place the banana, orange, mango, grapes, apple and coriander leaves in a serving bowl.
2 Mix the rest of the ingredients in a separate bowl until the sugar dissolves, then pour over the fruits and mix well.
3 Serve chilled with any Indian meal.

Raita is a yoghurt-based accompaniment that provides a cool, refreshing contrast to any spicy Indian meals. It can be prepared simply by adding any combination of diced vegetables like cucumber or tomato, chopped fresh herbs like mint or coriander, crushed seeds like cumin or coriander, or even sliced bananas to thick rich yoghurt.

Serves 4–6
Preparation time: **20 mins**

Punjabi Sweet Hot Mango Chutney

500 g (3 cups) grated
  peeled, ripe mango
1 tablespoon minced
  ginger
250 g (1 cup) sugar
2 teaspoons salt
1 1/2 teaspoons chilli
  powder
1 teaspoon *garam
  masala*
1/4 teaspoon citric acid
  crystals or powder
  (optional)

Serves 4–6
Preparation time: **15 mins**
Cooking time: **20 mins**

1 Put the grated mango and ginger into a saucepan and cook over low flame until all the juice has evaporated.
2 Add the sugar, salt, chilli powder, *garam masala* and citric acid crystals (if using), and cook over slow heat until the sugar dissolves and the chutney thickens.
3 Cool thoroughly before serving or storing in clean sterilized jars. The chutney can be used the next day, but is best served a week later. It can be stored in the fridge for 3 months.

Citric Acid is extracted from the juices of fruits and made into a white powder that is used as a flavouring in foods and beverages. It can also be produced by fermenting glucose, or by allowing water and molasses to ferment naturally.

Coriander Chutney

150 g (3 cups) chopped coriander leaves
2 green finger-length chillies
1 cm (¹/₂ in) ginger
2 tablespoons lemon juice
100 g (1 cup) grated coconut
4 tablespoons water
¹/₂ teaspoon salt

1 Put all the ingredients in a blender and process until very smooth.
2 Serve immediately or keep refrigerated until required.

Freshly grated coconut is available from Asian markets while desiccated (dried) coconut shavings are available from supermakets as well as many Asian foodstores.

Serves 4–6
Preparation time: **10 mins**

Tandoori Naan (Leavened Flat Bread)

250 g (1²/₃ cups) plain flour
100 ml (scant ¹/₂ cup) milk
1 tablespoon yoghurt
1¹/₄ teaspoons instant yeast
¹/₂ teaspoon sugar
¹/₂ teaspoon salt
3 tablespoons ghee or melted butter
1 tablespoon sesame seeds (optional)

Makes 4 *naan*
Preparation time: 30 mins + 2 hours standing time
Cooking time: 10 mins

1 Sift the flour into a bowl, then add the milk, yoghurt, yeast, sugar, salt and 1¹/₂ tablespoons of ghee or butter.
2 Mix, adding 1–2 more tablespoons milk if needed, until the dough becomes just too stiff to stir. Knead until the dough is soft and pliable, at least 10 minutes.
3 Cover the dough with a damp (not wet) cloth and set aside in a warm place until the dough doubles in size, about 1¹/₂–2 hours.
4 Preheat the oven to 190°C (375°F). Punch down the dough and divide it into 4 balls, then set the balls of dough aside for 10 minutes.
5 Roll out each ball of dough into a triangular shape, then pull out one side to make a teardrop shape.
6 Brush each piece with a little of the extra ghee, then sprinkle some sesame seeds on top, if using. Place on a baking tray and bake until puffed and golden brown, 5–10 minutes. Serve warm or at room temperature.

To make *badami naan* (almond flat bread), sprinkle 100 g slivered almonds on the naan after brushing with ghee in step 6. Follow the same baking instructions. For roghni naan (cream flat bread), replace milk with cream in the dough recipe.

Add the milk, yoghurt, yeast, ghee and salt to the sifted flour in the bowl.

Knead the dough until soft and pliable. Add extra milk if necessary.

Set aside until the dough doubles in size.

Roll into a triangle then pull one side to form a teardrop.

In a mixing bowl, combine all the stuffing ingredients.

Divide dough into 6 balls then, using thumb and fingers, form into a bowl.

10

Cauliflower Paratha (Unleavened Flat Bread)

250 g (2 cups) whole wheat (*atta*) flour
$^1/_2$ teaspoon salt
1 tablespoon butter or oil
200 ml ($^3/_4$ cup) plus 2 tablespoons water
250 g (1$^1/_4$ cup) cauliflower, grated
2 teaspoons lemon juice
$^1/_2$ teaspoon salt
4 tablespoons finely chopped coriander leaves
1 medium onion, finely chopped
1 green finger-length chilli, finely sliced
1 teaspoon finely minced fresh ginger root
Oil or ghee for shallow frying

Makes 6 *paratha*
Preparation time: 45 mins
Cooking time: 5 mins

1 Sift the flour and salt into a large basin and rub in the butter with your fingertips. Bring the flour together with the water to make a soft, pliable dough. Depending on the flour used, you may need a tablespoon or more of water. Knead until the dough is smooth and elastic, then cover and leave to rest for 30 minutes.

2 Meanwhile, make the filling. Put the grated cauliflower into a bowl and add enough hot water to cover. Put a lid on the bowl and set aside for 5 minutes. Drain in a sieve, pressing with a spoon to extract as much liquid as possible.

3 In a mixing bowl, combine the cauliflower, lemon juice, salt, coriander leaves, onion, chilli and ginger. Stir thoroughly and divide into 6 portions.

4 To assemble, knead the dough again and divide into 6 portions, each weighing about 70 g (2$^1/_3$ oz). Roll each portion into a ball, then using thumb and fingers, press the ball into a large bowl shape about 6 cm (2$^1/_2$ in) across. Place a portion of the cauliflower mixture into each dough bowl, then pinch the edges close. Try not to get the edges wet or they will be impossible to close. Shape into a ball again.

5 On a floured board, gently roll out the ball into a disc 13 cm (5 in) in diameter and $^3/_4$ cm ($^1/_4$ in) thick.

6 Shallow fry the disc on a hot griddle until both sides are golden brown in colour. Serve with a chutney.

Divide cauliflower mixture between dough bowls, then pinch the edges close.

Place paratha *on a floured board and gently roll into discs.*

Saffron Rice

2 tablespoons ghee or oil
5 cardamom pods
5 whole cloves
1 stick cinnamon, broken in half
1 bay leaf
1 medium onion, thinly sliced
1 green finger-length chilli, slit lengthwise
300 g (1 $^1/_2$ cups) basmati rice, washed, soaked
   for 30 mins and drained
500 ml (2 cups) water
Pinch saffron strands soaked in 60 ml ($^1/_4$ cup)
   hot milk
1 teaspoon salt

1 Heat the ghee or oil and fry the cardamom pods,
cloves, cinnamon and bay leaf until aromatic. Add the
rice and stir-fry for a few seconds until the rice grains
are coated with ghee.
2 Transfer to a rice cooker and add the remaining
ingredients. Stir to mix well.
3 Turn on the rice cooker and, when the rice is cooked,
remove the whole spices, fluff up the rice and serve with
curry and other accompaniments.

If you do not have a rice cooker, put the rice and spices
into a saucepan in step 2, add the remaining ingredients
and bring to a boil. Reduce the heat to low and simmer
until the rice is cooked.

Serves 4
Preparation time: **10 mins + 30 mins soaking time**
Cooking time: **25 mins**

Prawn Briyani (Fragrant Prawn Rice)

Rice
1 tablespoon ghee or oil
5 cardamom pods
5 whole cloves
1 stick cinnamon
1 bay leaf
300 g (1 1/2 cups)
  basmati rice, washed
  and soaked for 30 mins
  and drained
1 tablespoon lemon juice
2 green finger-length
  chillies, slit lengthwise
1 tablespoon ginger paste
1 tablespoon garlic paste
1 tablespoon rose water
50 ml (scant 1/4 cup)
  cream
1/2 teaspoon salt
Pinch saffron, crushed
500 ml (2 cups) water

Spice Paste
1 tablespoon ghee
  or oil
1 teaspoon oil
5 cardamom pods,
  seeds only
1 stick cinnamon, broken
  in half
5 whole cloves
2 bay leaves
2 tablespoons ginger
  paste
3 tablespoons garlic paste
1 medium tomato, finely
  chopped (about 1 cup)
1 medium onion, finely
  chopped (about 1 cup)
100 ml (scant 1/2 cup)
  yoghurt
1/2 teaspoon salt
1 teaspoon chilli powder

Prawns
500 g (1 lb) large
  prawns, shelled with
  tails intact
1 teaspoon *garam
  masala*

Serves 4
Preparation time: **25 mins**
Cooking time: **20 mins**

1 To prepare the Rice, heat the ghee or oil and fry the cardamon pods, cinnamon, cloves and bay leaf until aromatic. Stir in the drained rice and mix well so that the rice grains are coated with the spiced ghee. Transfer the rice mixture to a rice cooker.
2 Add in the rest of the Rice ingredients, mix well and turn on the rice cooker.
3 While the Rice is cooking, prepare the Spice Paste by heating the ghee or oil and frying the cardamon pods, cinnamon, cloves and bay leaves until aromatic. Add the ginger and garlic pastes, tomato and onion, and sauté until the tomato soften. Stir in the yoghurt, salt and chilli powder and cook until all the liquid has evaporated, about another 5 minutes.
4 Stir in the prawns and the *garam masala*, and stir fry until the prawns are cooked, about 3–4 minutes. Set aside and keep warm.
5 When the Rice is cooked, remove the whole spices, fluff up the rice and fold in the cooked prawns and Spice Paste. Serve hot.

Tomato and Green Mango Soup

2 tablespoons ghee or oil
1 teaspoon chopped ginger
1 teaspoon chopped garlic
1 teaspoon coriander seeds
2 tablespoons plain flour blended with 125 ml
  ($^1/_2$ cup) water
200 g (1 cup) unripe green mango flesh, peeled and
  finely chopped
500 g ($2^1/_2$ cups) finely chopped ripe tomatoes or
  canned tomatoes
$1^1/_2$ litres (6 cups) stock or water
2 bay leaves
$1^1/_4$ teaspoons salt
$^1/_2$ teaspoon ground white pepper
Chopped coriander leaves, as garnish

1 Heat the ghee or oil in a medium stockpot and sauté
the ginger, garlic and coriander seeds until aromatic.
2 Add in the rest of the ingredients and boil for about
10 minutes over low flame.
3 Remove from the heat and cool a little before pouring
the soup into a blender to blend until smooth.
4 Strain back into the saucepan and reheat. Garnish
with the chopped coriander leaves and serve.

Serves 4
Preparation time: 25 mins
Cooking time: 30 mins

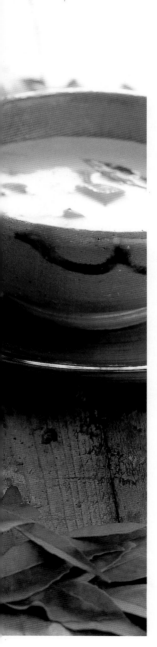

Yoghurt Soup

2 teaspoons channa flour
125 ml ($^1/_2$ cup) water
$^1/_4$ teaspoon ground white pepper
1 teaspoon salt
$^1/_2$ teaspoon turmeric powder
$^1/_2$ teaspoon curry powder
1 tablespoon ghee or butter
1 tablespoon oil
1 teaspoon fenugreek seeds
1 teaspoon mustard seeds
1 sprig curry leaves
150 g (1$^1/_2$ cups) white daikon radish, cubed
1 litre (4 cups) water
3 tablespoons cream
150 ml ($^2/_3$ cup) plain yoghurt, beaten

1 Pour the water into a measuring cup, then stir in the channa flour. Add the pepper, salt, turmeric and curry powders and set aside.
2 Heat the ghee or butter and oil and fry the fenugreek and mustard seeds until they crackle. Add the curry leaves.
3 Stir in the channa flour mixture, radish and water. Cook over medium-high heat until the radish is soft when pierced with the tip of a knife, about 30 minutes.
4 Add the cream and yoghurt and turn off the heat. Stir to mix well and serve the soup hot or warm.

Serves 4
Preparation time: **10 mins**
Cooking time: **40 mins**

Mixed Vegetable Curry

1 tablespoon butter or oil
3 green finger-length chillies, slit lengthwise
2 medium carrots diced (about 1 1/2 cups)
1 large or 2 small potatoes, peeled and diced
200 g (1 cup) diced pumpkin
200 g (2 cups) cauliflower, cut into pieces
200 g (1 1/2 cups) French beans, cut into pieces
75 g (1/2 cup) fresh or frozen green peas
150 ml (2/3 cup) cream
1 tablespoon dried fenugreek leaves (optional)
3 tablespoons finely chopped coriander leaves

Tomato Sauce
2 tablespoons butter or oil
3 tablespoons ginger paste
3 tablespoons garlic paste
3 medium or 5 small ripe tomatoes, chopped and 1 can (240g/8 oz) peeled tomatoes
1 teaspoon salt, or to taste
2–3 teaspoons chilli powder
200 ml (3/4 cup) water

1 To prepare the Tomato Sauce, heat the butter or oil in a wok or saucepan and stir-fry the ginger and garlic pastes. Add the fresh tomatoes, salt, chilli powder and fry until soft. Add the canned tomatoes and water. Cover and simmer until the tomatoes are very soft and mushy, about 15 minutes.

2 Cool the Tomato Sauce, then puree in a blender and set aside.

3 Heat the butter or oil in a wok. Sauté the chillies, then add the diced carrots, potatoes and cook for 15–20 minutes, adding the Tomato Sauce to the vegetables. When the carrots are softened, add the pumpkin, cauliflower, French beans and green peas. Simmer until all the vegetables are cooked through, about another 10 minutes.

4 Stir in the cream, fenugreek leaves, if using, and coriander. Remove from the heat, mix thoroughly and serve.

If **fenugreek leaves** are not available, you can sprout your own by soaking a tablespoon of fenugreek for a couple of hours, then sprouting them on damp paper towels. When the shoots are about 3–4 cm (1 1/2 in), they can be used. Alternatively, grind 1/2 teaspoon fenugreek seeds and use them in place of the leaves.

Serves 6
Preparation time: **30 mins**
Cooking time: **45 mins**

Curried Baby Potatoes

500 g (1 lb) baby potatoes
Oil for frying
1 teaspoon cumin seeds
1 teaspoon coriander
   seeds
2 whole cloves
2 black cardamom pods,
   seeds only (optional)
1 tablespoon grated
   coconut
Pinch of mace (see note)
60 g (1/3 cup) blanched
   almonds
2 in (5 cm) ginger, sliced
4 cloves garlic, peeled
4 green finger-length
   chillies, seeded and
   sliced
100 ml (scant 1/2 cup)
   water
2 tablespoons ghee or oil
1 small onion, finely
   chopped
1 teaspoon chilli powder
1/2 teaspoon turmeric
   powder
150 ml (2/3 cup) plain
   yoghurt
1 teaspoon salt
250 ml (1 cup) water
2 tablespoons finely
   chopped coriander
   leaves

1 Wash the potatoes well and prick all over with a fork. Heat the oil and fry the potatoes until golden, 5–10 minutes. Remove, drain and set aside.

2 Dry roast the cumin, coriander, cloves and cardamom seeds, coconut and mace until aromatic.

3 Put the roasted ingredients into a blender with the almonds, garlic, ginger, chillies and the 1/2 cup water and blend to a smooth paste.

4 In a clean pan, heat the ghee or oil and sauté the onions until golden brown, about 5 minutes. Add the blended ingredients, chilli and turmeric powders and fry over high heat for 1–2 minutes. Reduce the heat, then slowly stir in the yoghurt.

5 Add the fried potatoes and salt, and cook for 2–3 minutes, stirring occasionally to prevent the mixture from sticking.

6 Add 250ml (1 cup) water and mix gently. Increase the heat and bring to a boil, then reduce the heat and simmer until the sauce thickens, about 10 minutes.

7 Remove from the heat and serve, garnished with the coriander leaves.

Mace is the dried wrapping that covers the nutmeg seed. Its flavour is similar to nutmeg, but slightly more bitter. It is usually sold in ground form, but is sometimes available in whole blades. It can be substituted with nutmeg or cinnamon.

Serves 4
Preparation time: **15 mins**
Cooking time: **35 mins**

Sweet and Sour Eggplant

3 heaping tablespoons (70 g) tamarind pulp soaked in
375 ml (1$^1/_2$ cups) water
4 long purple eggplants (brinjals), about 750 g (1$^1/_2$ lbs)
250 ml (1 cup) mustard oil or vegetable oil
5 whole cloves
5 cardamom pods
2 green finger-length chillies, slit lengthwise
2 teaspoons chilli powder
$^1/_2$ teaspoon turmeric powder
$^1/_2$ teaspoon cumin powder
1 tablespoon fennel powder
1 teaspoon *garam masala*
50 g ($^1/_4$ cup) caster sugar
Salt to taste

1 Stir, mash and strain the tamarind pulp, discarding
the solids, to obtain the juice.
2 Cut the eggplants into quarters lengthwise, then
into 4 cm (1$^1/_2$ in) lengths.
3 Heat the oil in a wok and fry the eggplants until half
cooked. Drain and set aside.
4 Discard all but 2 tablespoons of the oil and fry
the cloves, cardamom pods and green chillies
until aromatic.
5 Add in the ground spice powders, salt and sugar,
tamarind juice as well as the fried eggplant. Cook
until the gravy has thickened and the eggplant tender.

Serves 4
Preparation time: **15 mins**
Cooking time: **15 mins**

Fragrant Dal Curry

200 g (1 cup) mixed dal
(equal portions of red,
split, mung, *urad* and
pigeon lentils)
1¹/₄ litres (5 cups) water
1 teaspoon salt
1 teaspoon chilli powder
1 teaspoon turmeric
powder
2 tablespoons ghee or oil
1 teaspoon cumin seeds
5 cm (2 in) fresh ginger,
cut into very fine strips
(to yield 2 tablespoons)
1 small ripe tomato, diced
2 tablespoons chopped
coriander leaves

1 Wash the lentils and place in a pot together with the water, salt, chilli and turmeric powder. Boil and simmer until the lentils are soft.
2 In a separate pan, heat the ghee or oil and fry the cumin seeds until aromatic. Add in the ginger strips and tomatoes and sauté until the tomatoes become soft.
3 Transfer to the boiling dal; add in the chopped coriander leaves and continue to simmer for another 2 minutes. Turn off the heat and serve.

Serves 4
Preparation time: **10 mins**
Cooking time: **45 mins**

Tandoori Cauliflower

800 g (1³/₄ lbs) cauli-
flower florets
1 teaspoon salt
2 tablespoons ginger
paste
2 tablespoons garlic
paste
2 teaspoons chilli powder
1 teaspoon *garam
masala*
2 tablespoons lemon juice
140 g (¹/₂ cup plus
2 tablespoons) channa
flour
250 ml (1 cup) water
³/₄ teaspoon salt
Oil for deep-frying
Ghee or oil for basting

1 Cut the cauliflower into medium-sized florets.
Wash and drain thoroughly.
2 Stir the salt, ginger and garlic pastes, chilli powder,
garam masala and lemon juice together and toss with
the cauliflower florets in this mix. Set aside to
marinate for 1 hour.
3 Mix the channa flour, water and salt to make a
thick batter.
4 Heat the oil. Dip the marinated cauliflower, floret
by floret, into the batter then deep-fry until lightly
browned. Remove and drain on paper towels.
5 Carefully place the fried cauliflower on skewers and
grill on a gas or charcoal grill or bake in a very hot oven
(230°C/450°F) until golden brown, about 4–6 minutes.
Baste with ghee or oil while grilling or baking.

Serves 6
Preparation time: 15 mins + 1 hour marinating time
Cooking time: 40 mins

Baked Fish with Cashew Nuts and Spices

1 kg (2 lbs) whole white fish, (like seabass or pomfret) cleaned, washed and wiped dry

5 tablespoons ginger paste

5 tablespoons garlic paste

$1/2$ teaspoon salt

1 tablespoon lemon juice

250 ml (1 cup) oil

1 medium onion, finely grated and mixed with a little water to form a paste

50 g ($1/3$ cup) ground cashew nuts

$1 1/4$ teaspoons chilli powder

$1/2$ teaspoon turmeric powder

1 teaspoon salt

2 teaspoons coriander powder

1 teaspoon fenugreek powder

2 teaspoons *garam masala*

150 ml ($2/3$ cup) plain yoghurt

375 ml ($1 1/2$ cups) hot water

1 Combine 3 tablespoons of the ginger paste, 3 tablespoons of the garlic paste, salt and lemon juice and mix well. Rub over the fish and set aside for 1 hour.

2 Preheat the oven to 150°C (300°F).

3 In a large frying pan or wok, heat the oil until very hot and fry the marinated fish until half cooked.

4 Drain the fish and place in an ovenproof dish.

5 Spoon 4 tablespoons of the oil into a saucepan and sauté the remaining ginger and garlic pastes, and onion paste, until lightly browned. Stir in the remaining ingredients except the hot water and cook on low heat until the oil separates.

6 Add the hot water to the spice paste and bring the gravy to a boil for 5 minutes. Pour the gravy over the fish and bake in the preheated oven for 30 minutes, basting the fish at regular intervals with the gravy.

Serves 4
Preparation time: **15 mins + 1 hour standing time**
Cooking time: **1 hour**

Fish Kofta Curry (Fish Ball Curry)

400 g (14 oz) fish
  fillet, skin and bones
  removed, minced
3/4 teaspoon salt
2 green finger-length
  chillies, finely chopped
2 cloves garlic, finely
  minced
1/2 teaspoon turmeric
  powder
2 teaspoons channa flour
4 tablespoons oil
8 cardamom pods
1 teaspoon cumin seeds
3 medium onions, thinly
  sliced
2 tablespoons ginger
  paste
3 tablespoons garlic
  paste
1 teaspoon chilli powder
1 teaspoon turmeric
  powder
1 teaspoon *garam
  masala*
5 tablespoons tomato
  purée
250 ml (1 cup) cream or
  unsweetened evapo-
  rated milk
250 ml (1 cup) water
3/4 teaspoon salt

1 Combine the minced fish, salt, chillies, garlic, turmeric powder and channa flour in a mixing bowl. Mix well and shape into balls 2 cm (3/4 in) in diameter. Set aside.
2 Heat the oil in a medium saucepan and fry the cardamom pods and cumin seeds until aromatic. Add in the onion slices, ginger and garlic pastes and sauté until golden brown.
3 Add the spice powders and the tomato purée and sauté over low heat until the oil separates, about 1 minute. Stir in the cream or evaporated milk and water, season with the salt and bring the curry to a boil.
4 Gently lower the prepared fish balls into the curry and simmer over medium heat until the fish balls are cooked and float to the top, about 10 minutes.

Serves 4–6
Preparation time: 30 mins
Cooking time: 25 mins

Bengali Fish Curry

500 g (1 lb) fish cutlets or steaks
4 tablespoons oil
$^1/_2$ teaspoon cumin seeds
$^1/_4$ teaspoon fenugreek
$^1/_4$ teaspoon fennel seeds
$^1/_4$ teaspoon mustard seeds
3 tablespoons ginger paste
3 tablespoons garlic paste
3 tablespoons green chilli paste
1 teaspoon turmeric powder
3 tablespoons mustard seeds, ground
200 ml (scant 1 cup) water
1 teaspoon salt

1 Heat half the oil and fry the fish slices for 3 minutes on both sides. Drain and set aside with the oil and the juice.

2 In a large saucepan or wok, heat the remaining oil and fry the cumin, fenugreek, fennel and mustard seeds until aromatic. Add in the rest of the ingredients except for the fried fish slices and cook for 5 minutes, stirring often.

3 When the gravy bubbles, gently lower the fish slices into the pan and simmer for 3 minutes. Remove and serve.

Serves 4
Preparation time: **10 mins**
Cooking time: **25 mins**

Punjabi Fish Curry

800 g (1³/₄ lbs) fish fillets
¹/₂ teaspoon salt
1 teaspoon turmeric powder
2 tablespoons lemon juice
7 tablespoons oil
1 teaspoon mustard seeds
2 sprigs curry leaves
2 medium onions, finely chopped (about 2 cups)
2 teaspoons finely chopped ginger
3 ripe medium tomatoes, diced (about 2¹/₂ cups)
1¹/₂ teaspoons chilli powder
2 teaspoons coriander powder
1 teaspoon cumin powder
¹/₂ teaspoon turmeric powder
250 ml (1 cup) yoghurt
125 ml (¹/₂ cup) water
¹/₂ teaspoon salt
2 tablespoons coriander leaves

1 Rub the salt, 1 teaspoon turmeric powder and lemon juice on the fish slices and set aside for 20 minutes.
2 Heat 5 tablespoons of the oil and fry the fish slices for 2–3 minutes on each side. Drain on paper towels and set aside.
3 In a clean saucepan, heat the remaining oil and fry the mustard seeds and curry leaves until the mustard seeds splutter. Add the onions and ginger and sauté until the onion is lightly browned, about 5 minutes.
4 Add the tomatoes, chilli powder, coriander, cumin and ¹/₂ teaspoon turmeric powder and the yoghurt and fry over low heat until the oil separates. Add the water and salt and bring to a boil.
5 Add the fried fish to the curry and cook over low heat for 3–4 minutes.
6 Serve garnished with the coriander leaves.

Serves 4
Preparation time: **10 mins + 20 mins standing time**
Cooking time: **25 mins**

Prawn Kurma with Almonds and Cashews

500 g (1 lb) large prawns, shelled and deveined
3 tablespoons oil
3 cardamom pods
1 star anise
3 medium onions, finely chopped (about 3 cups)
1 tablespoon ginger paste
1 tablespoon garlic paste
1 teaspoon turmeric powder
1 teaspoon chilli powder
1 teaspoon coriander powder
1 teaspoon cumin powder
1 teaspoon *garam masala*
2 large or 3 medium ripe sweet tomatoes, blanched, skinned and chopped (or use canned chopped tomatoes)
$1/2$ teaspoon sugar
1 teaspoon salt
100 ml (scant $1/2$ cup) cream
2 tablespoons toasted almond flakes
2 tablespoons toasted cashew nuts, broken
1 tablespoon raisins
2 tablespoons chopped coriander leaves

1 Heat the oil and fry the cardamom pods and star anise until aromatic. Add the onions and sauté until golden brown, 5–10 minutes.

2 Stir in the ginger and garlic pastes, turmeric, chilli, coriander, cumin and *garam masala* powders and the chopped tomatoes and continue stirring over low heat until the oil separates.

3 Add the remaining ingredients and cook, covered, stirring occasionally, until the prawns are cooked, about 10 minutes.

Serves 4
Preparation time: **20 mins**
Cooking time: **25 mins**

Masala Prawns

500 g (1 lb) large
  prawns, shelled
3 tablespoons oil
2 teaspoons cumin seeds
3 medium onions, finely
  chopped
3 tablespoons ginger
  paste
3 tablespoons garlic
  paste
2 tablespoons lemon
  juice or vinegar
1 tablespoon grated
  palm sugar or brown
  sugar
3 ripe medium tomatoes,
  finely chopped
1 teaspoon *garam
  masala*
1 teaspoons chilli
  powder
1 teaspoon turmeric
  powder
$1/2$ teaspoon nutmeg
  powder
$1/2$ teaspoon freshly
  ground black pepper
$1 1/4$ teaspoons salt
2 tablespoons finely
  chopped coriander
  leaves

1 Heat the oil and fry the cumin seeds until aromatic. Add the onions and sauté until golden brown, 5–10 minutes.

2 Stir in the remaining ingredients except for the prawns and coriander leaves and continue cooking over low heat until the oil separates.

3 Add the prawns and stir to mix well. Cover and leave to simmer until the prawns are cooked through, about 10 minutes.

4 Sprinkle with the chopped coriander leaves and serve.

Serves 4
Preparation time: 30 mins
Cooking time: 20 mins

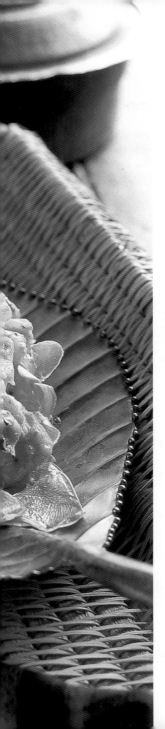

Tandoori Lobster

4 medium lobsters
2 tablespoons oil
4 tablespoons ghee or butter for basting

Marinade 1
2 tablespoons ginger paste
2 tablespoons garlic paste
1 teaspoon carom seeds
1 teaspoon salt
4 tablespoons lemon juice

Marinade 2
$3^1/_2$ tablespoons channa flour
$1^1/_2$ teaspoons chilli powder
$^1/_2$ teaspoon turmeric powder
2 teaspoons *garam masala*
250 ml (1 cup) plain yoghurt
1 egg, lightly beaten
$^3/_4$ teaspoon salt
60 g ($^1/_4$ cup) cottage cheese (*paneer*)

1 Shell and devein the lobsters and cut the meat into large cubes. Reserve the shells.
2 Prepare Marinade 1 by stirring together all the ingredients in a bowl. Add the lobster meat and marinate for 1 hour.
3 Clean, wash and drain the lobster shells. Heat the oil in a pan and fry the lobster shells until pink and fragrant, then set aside.
4 Combine the ingredients for Marinade 2 in a bowl and mix well to form a paste. Rub the paste onto the lobster meat and marinate, refrigerated, for a further 3–5 hours.
5 Preheat the oven to 220°C (425°F). Skewer the lobster meat about 2 cm ($^3/_4$ in) apart and roast for about 10 minutes, basting occasionally with ghee or butter.
6 When the meat is ready, remove from the skewers and serve in the prepared lobster shells.

Serves 4
Preparation time: 20 mins + 5–6 hours marinating time
Cooking time: 15 mins

Tandoori Chicken Breasts

4 large chicken breasts
(about 600 g/1$\frac{1}{4}$ lbs),
skin removed, 3 deep
cuts made on each side
1 green finger-length
chilli, finely sliced
Ghee or oil for
basting

Marinade
2 teaspoons chilli powder
2 tablespoons lemon juice
7 tablespoons heavy
cream
250 ml (1 cup) plain
yoghurt
3 tablespoons ginger paste
3 tablespoons garlic paste
1 teaspoon ground cumin
2 teaspoons *garam
masala*
$\frac{1}{2}$ teaspoon salt
1 teaspoon freshly
ground black pepper
Pinch of saffron, crushed,
1 teaspoon turmeric
powder

1 Spoon the lemon juice over the chicken, sprinkle the chilli powder over them, and rub both into the meat. Set aside.

2 Combine all the other Marinade ingredients in a bowl and mix until smooth. Add the chicken and work the Marinade into the chicken, making sure all pieces are evenly coated. Marinate for 4–5 hours in the refrigerator, or overnight.

3 Preheat the oven to 180°C (350°F).

4 Place the chicken on a roasting pan and cook in the oven for 15 minutes. Baste with ghee or oil, turn the chicken pieces over and roast the other side for another 10 minutes or until the chicken is cooked.

5 Serve with slices of finely sliced green chillies.

Serves 4
Preparation time: **10 mins + 7 hours standing time**
Cooking time: **25 mins**

Chicken Tikka

600 g (1¼ lbs) chicken breast, cubed
Oil or ghee for basting
24 bamboo skewers

Marinade
4 tablespoons plain yoghurt
3 tablespoons garlic paste
3 tablespoons ginger paste
4 tablespoons lemon juice
1 tablespoon channa flour
1 teaspoon ground cumin
½ teaspoon ground cardamom seeds
1 teaspoon chilli powder
½ teaspoon ground turmeric
½ teaspoon *garam masala*
1 teaspoon salt

1 In a large mixing bowl, stir together all the ingredients
for the Marinade to form a smooth mixture. Add the
chicken cubes, mix well and leave to marinate for
3 to 5 hours in the refrigerator.
2 Skewer the chicken cubes and roast in a hot oven or
tandoor for 5 minutes. Baste with oil or ghee and roast
a further 5 minutes.

Serves 4
Preparation time: 10 mins + 3 hours standing time
Cooking time: 20–25 mins

Butter Chicken

1 portion Chicken Tikka
(page 44)
125 g (6 tablespoons)
butter
1 stick cinnamon, broken
in half
8 cardamom pods
2 bay leaves
3 tablespoons ginger
paste
1 tablespoon garlic paste
3 large or 5 medium ripe
sweet tomatoes,
chopped
375 ml (1$^1/_2$ cups) water
1$^1/_2$ teaspoons salt
2$^1/_2$ cm (1 in) fresh ginger,
cut into very fine strips
4 green finger-length
chillies, seeded and slit
lengthwise
1 teaspoon chilli powder
1 tablespoon honey
125 ml ($^1/_2$ cup) cream
2 tablespoons chopped
coriander leaves

1 Prepare the Chicken Tikka by following the recipe on page 44.

2 Heat half of the butter in a pan and fry the cinnamon sticks, cardamom pods and bay leaves until aromatic. Stir in the ginger and garlic pastes and sauté until the juice evaporates and the paste is dry. Add the tomatoes, water and salt and boil for about 15 minutes or until the tomatoes are soft. Mash and strain the mixture through a sieve and set aside.

3 In another pan, heat the remaining butter and sauté the ginger strips and chillies. Add the strained tomato gravy, chilli powder and the prepared Chicken Tikka pieces. Simmer for 15 minutes or until the chicken is tender.

4 Stir in the cream and honey and mix well. Remove from the heat and serve, garnished with the coriander leaves.

Serves 4
Preparation time: 15 mins + 3$^1/_2$ hours for the Chicken Tikka
Cooking time: 40 mins

Lemon Masala Chicken

675 g (1 1/2 lbs) chicken breasts, cut into bite-sized cubes
2 medium onions, thickly sliced
1 medium green bell peppers, cut into rings
1 medium red bell peppers, cut into rings
2 tablespoons butter or ghee

Marinade
150 ml (2/3 cup) plain yoghurt
2 tablespoon ginger paste
2 tablespoons garlic paste
3 tablespoons ground almonds or cashew nuts
Pinch of saffron, crushed and soaked in 2 tablespoons hot milk
1 teaspoon cumin seeds
1 teaspoon salt
5 green finger-length chillies, chopped
3 tablespoons lemon juice
1 teaspoon freshly ground black pepper

1 To make the Marinade, combine all the ingredients in a medium bowl and stir to form a smooth paste. Add the chicken pieces and marinate for 2 hours.
2 Preheated the oven to 180°C (350°F). Remove the chicken pieces from the Marinade and place in a single layer in a greased ovenproof dish. Arrange the sliced onion and bell pepper rings over the chicken and spoon the remaining Marinade evenly over the top.
3 Dot with teaspoons of butter or ghee and bake until the chicken is cooked, about 35 minutes. To test if the chicken is cooked, insert a skewer into a piece of chicken. It is done if the juices run clear.
4 Remove from the oven and serve hot.

Serves 4
Preparation time: 20 mins + 2 hours marinating time
Cooking time: 35 mins

Kastoori Chicken

675 g (1 1/2 lbs) chicken, cut into bite-sized cubes

150 ml (2/3 cup) plain yoghurt

1 teaspoon turmeric powder

1/2 teaspoon salt

2 tablespoons oil

5 whole cloves

5 cardamom pods

1 teaspoon cumin seeds

2 bay leaves

2 medium onions, finely chopped

3 tablespoons ginger paste

3 tablespoons garlic paste

4 tablespoons onion paste

80 g (2/3 cup) cashew nuts, ground to yield about 10 tablespoons

2 teaspoons coriander powder

2 teaspoons chilli powder

1 teaspoon salt

2 tablespoons fenugreek, soaked in half cup (125 ml) water for 30 minutes (see Note)

1/2 teaspoon *garam masala*

3 cm (1 1/4 in) ginger, cut into fine strips

1 medium tomato, sliced

2 tablespoons chopped coriander leaves

1 Marinate the chicken pieces in the yoghurt, turmeric and salt for 1 hour.

2 Heat the oil in a large saucepan or wok and fry the cloves, cardamom pods, cumin seeds and bay leaves until fragrant. Add the chopped onions and sauté until golden brown.

3 Add the ginger, garlic and onion pastes and sauté for a further 1 minute.

4 Stir in the rest of the ingredients, return the chicken and marinade to the pan, and cook until the chicken is tender, about 20 to 30 minutes.

If **fenugreek leaves** are not available, you can sprout your own by soaking a tablespoon of fenugreek for a couple of hours, then sprouting them on damp paper towels. When the shoots are about 3 4 cm (1 1/2 in), they can be used. Alternatively, grind 1/2 teaspoon fenugreek seeds and use them in place of the leaves.

Serves 4
Preparation time: **10 mins + 1 hour standing time**
Cooking time: **30 mins**

Minced Lamb in Yoghurt Curry

1 litre (4 cups) water
675 g (1 1/2 lbs) minced
  lamb
3 tablespoons ginger
3 tablespoons garlic
2 bay leaves
4 sticks cinnamon
3 tablespoons oil
5 cardamom pods
5 whole cloves
2 onions, finely chopped
2 green chillies, slit
  lengthwise
1 large or 2 small ripe
  tomatoes, diced
150 ml (2/3 cup)
  plain yoghurt
4 tablespoons cashew
  nut paste
1 teaspoon turmeric
  powder
1 teaspoon cumin
  powder
2 teaspoons coriander
  powder
2 teaspoons chilli
  powder
1 teaspoon *garam
  masala*
1 1/2 teaspoons salt
4 tablespoons chopped
  coriander leaves
150 g (1 cup) peas
1 medium potato, peeled
  and finely diced

1 Place the water, lamb, ginger and garlic pastes, bay leaves and 2 cinnamon sticks in a pot. Bring to a boil and cook for 10 minutes, stirring frequently.

2 In a large pot, heat the oil and fry the remaining 2 cinnamon sticks, cardamom pods and cloves until aromatic, then add in the onion and chillies. Sauté until the onion turns golden brown.

3 Add the rest of the ingredients to the pot together with the cooked lamb and simmer until the potatoes are cooked, about 50 minutes.

Serves 4
Preparation time: **20 mins**
Cooking time: **1 hour**

Lamb in Thick Almond Gravy

750 g (1 1/2 lbs) boneless
  lamb, cubed
3 tablespoons oil
7 cardamom pods
5 whole cloves
2 sticks cinnamon
2 bay leaves
3 black cardamom pods
2 onions, peeled and
  sliced
90 g (3/4 cup) raw
  almonds, ground
3 tablespoons ginger
  paste
3 tablespoons garlic paste
3/4 teaspoon salt
1 teaspoon freshly ground
  black pepper
1 teaspoon salt
1 litre (4 cups) water
200 ml (3/4 cup) pome-
  granate or grape juice
4 tablespoons cream

Marinade
3 tablespoons ginger
  paste
3 tablespoons garlic paste
1 teaspoon chilli powder
1 teaspoon salt
100 ml (1/2 cup) plain
  yoghurt

1 Combine all the Marinade ingredients in a bowl.
Add the lamb and mix well. Marinate for at least
3 hours in the refrigerator.
2 Heat the oil and fry the cardamom pods, cloves,
cinnamon, bay leaves and black cardamom pods until
aromatic. Add the sliced onions and fry until golden
brown, about 5 minutes.
3 Add the remaining ingredients, except the cream,
and bring to a boil. Lower the heat and simmer until
the lamb is tender and the gravy is thick, about
45 minutes.
4 Remove from the heat, stir in the cream and serve.

Serves 4–6
Preparation time: 20 mins + 3 hours marinating time
Cooking time: 1 hour

Spicy Pork Chops

5 medium pork chops
(800 g or 1$^3/_4$ lbs),
sliced into thin cutlets
7 green finger-length
chillies, sliced
100 g (2$^1/_2$ cups) mint
leaves, roughly chopped
(reserve some whole
for the garnish)
100 g (2$^1/_2$ cups)
coriander leaves,
roughly chopped
1 medium tomato,
quartered
180 ml ($^3/_4$ cup) water
4 tablespoons oil
2 sticks cinnamon
5 whole cloves
5 cardamom pods
1$^1/_2$ teaspoons fennel
seeds
1 medium onion, sliced
3 tablespoons ginger paste
3 tablespoons garlic paste
2 tablespoons coriander
powder
600 ml (2$^1/_2$ cups) water
1 teaspoon salt

1 Process the chillies, mint and coriander leaves, tomatoes and 180 ml ($^3/_4$ cup) water until smooth.

2 Heat the oil in a wok or saucepan and fry the cinnamon, cloves, cardamom pods and fennel until aromatic. Add the onions and sauté until golden brown, about 5 minutes.

3 Add the pork chops and cook both sides until lightly coloured, about10 minutes.

4 Add the remaining ingredients and simmer over medium heat until the pork chops are tender and the gravy is so thick that it coats the chops, about 1 hour. Serve garnished with the reserved mint leaves.

Serves 5
Preparation time: 20 mins
Cooking time: 1 hour 30 mins

Mango Ice-cream

750 ml (3 cups) full
  cream milk
300 ml (1¹/₄ cups) cream
300 ml (1¹/₄ cups)
  evaporated milk
300 ml (1¹/₄ cups)
  sweetened condensed
  milk
4 tablespoons caster sugar
¹/₄ teaspoon cardamom
  powder
1 large ripe mango,
  peeled and blended
  (about 1¹/₄ cups)

1 Put the full cream milk, cream, evaporated milk,
condensed milk and sugar into a heavy bottomed
3 litre (3 quart) pot. Bring to a boil, stirring
constantly, making sure to scrape the bottom of the
pan to avoid scorching.
2 Simmer for about 30 minutes or until the milk is
reduced in volume by half.
3 Cool the mixture thoroughly before folding in the
ground cardamoms and mango pulp. Combine well.
4 Pour into *kulfi* moulds or ice cube trays or a shallow
metal freezing container.
5 Cover and freeze until firm, about 7–10 hours.

Serves 6
Preparation time: 10 mins
Cooking time: 45 mins + 7–10 hours freezing time

Sweet Lassi

500 ml (2 cups)
  plain yoghurt
100 g ($^1/_2$ cup) sugar
  (according to taste)
1 litre (4 cups) cool water
Ice cubes
$^1/_4$ teaspoon cardamom
  powder

1 In a large jug, combine the yoghurt, sugar and water until smooth. Check the seasoning, then refrigerate to chill.
2 To serve, put ice cubes into a glass, pour in the lassi mixture and top with a sprinkle of freshly ground cardamon powder.

Serves 4
Preparation time: **5 mins**
Chilling time: **1 hour**

Index